Indefinite Detention:

A Dog Story

MICHAEL ROTHENBERG

Indefinite Detention: A Dog Story

Copyright © 2013, 2014 by Michael Rothenberg

All rights reserved. No part of this book may be reproduced or transmitted in any form or by any means without written permission of the author.

ISBN: 978-0-9853151-6-0

Library of Congress Control Number: 2013943683

Cover design by Terri Carrion

Thanks to Albrechto Alvarez, Andrew Topel, and Lewis Warsh for their work and inspiration in creation of the book cover collage.

Published by Shabda Press
Pasadena, CA 91107

for Terri

The dog trots freely in the street and sees reality and the things he sees are bigger than himself...

~ Lawrence Ferlinghetti

Some of these poems have previously appeared in *3:AM Magazine, Beehive, Court Green, House Organ, Otoliths, Golden Handcuffs Review, kihupotru, Isibongo, Penumbra, The Blue Jew Yorker, Ygdrasil* and *OR*. "Ode to Tralfamadorian Goose" was selected for the PIP Gertrude Stein Awards for Innovative Poetry in English 2005-2006 (Green Integer Press). "Maybe I Want To Go To Canada" first appeared in *From Somewhere to Nowhere: The End of the American Dream,* Unbearable Books/Autonomedia, 2012. "Day 4" appeared in Polish trans. in *LiteRacje's Anthropology of Curiosity Issue* (2010). Portions of "Head Shed" first appeared in the chapbook *Epigenesis On Temple Mount* (dPress, Sebastopol, CA 2006).

Special thanks to Teresa Mei Chuc, David Madgalene, Neeli Cherkovski, Youssef Alaoui, Dennis Dybeck, and Jim Spitzer.

Contents

1
Maybe I Want To Go To Canada...3

2
Indefinite Detention: A Dog Story..7
Moving With Terri...16
Dancer..17
The Sewing Machine: The Perfect Art..18
Ode to Tralfamadorian Goose..22
Groggy..26
Poem For Mitko..27

3
Head Shed...35

4
The Book...49

5

Track 77

6

Gray Days 105

End Of January 113

Day 4 116

Morning Noise. 118

Anxiety 120

New Day 122

Broken 124

Scaffolding. 128

About the Author. 131

1

Maybe I Want To Go To Canada

Bye, Bye USA. Hello Finland! Or maybe I want to go to Canada. . . I'm fresh out of patriotism. Tired of disappointment and hurt. I need a bigger world view. O, Samsara! Let it go, let it go! Ziggy, my dog, sleeps in the sun. Everything will work out here at home. But no, there are 17 countries more Democratic than this one. I want to go there!

That would be the brave and honorable thing to do. Emigrate! A vote for Democracy while I still have a chance to vote. It would be just like going to America. But backwards when America was determined to be America. Hello Sweden! I'll have a hotdog with mashed potatoes, mustard and ketchup, at the train station. I'll have a beautiful blonde

girl! It doesn't matter where as long as I'm free. Hello better democracies! Norway, Iceland, Netherlands, Denmark, New Zealand, Switzerland, Luxembourg, Australia, Canada, Iceland, Germany, Austria, Spain, Malta, Japan. Tapas, herring, moose and kangaroos, fondue, tempura, great forests and Northern Lights. Hello Leonard

Cohen, I'm on my way! Health care, free speech, civil rights! And what about Gross National Happiness? Physical, mental and spiritual health! The USA ranks 150! Behind Costa Rica, Dominican Republic, and Vietnam, just to get started. Fer Christ's Sake they're happier in Saudi Arabia! And which country is the greenest? The USA ranks 39th behind Switzerland, Sweden, Norway, Finland, Costa Rica, orchids, bromeliads, parrots. Mambas, Sambas, Cha-Chas. Austria, New Zealand, Latvia, Colombia, France, Iceland, Björk, haddock, halibut, and shrimp. Canada, Germany, lederhosen, United Kingdom, Slovenia, klobasa, strudels, goulash and pancakes topped with chocolate, Lithuania,

Slovakia, Portugal, Estonia, Croatia, Japan, Ecuador, Hungary, Italy. Risotto, fava, white truffles and fresh parmesan. "Maestà" by Duccio di Buoninsegna at Museo dell'Opera del Duomo, Siena. Denmark, Malaysia, Albania, Russia, Chile, Roberto Matta, empanada de Pino filled with diced meat, onions, olive, raisins and a piece of hard-boiled egg.

Cabernet Sauvignon, and Pablo Neruda, Spain, Lorca, Don Quixote, Luxembourg, Panama, Dominican Republic, Ireland, Brazil, Gooooooooooooooooooooooooal!!!!!!!!! Uruguay, Georgia and Argentina, Water purity, lower carbon and sulfur emissions… Long live the glaciers, waterfalls, coral reefs, flowering meadows, mangroves, and fjords!

Before it's too late. What am I waiting for? I've got to do what's right (for me). It's the American thing to do! I've go to get out of here. All aboard for A Happy Green Democracy! That's what I imagine. That's what I choose!

2

Indefinite Detention: A Dog Story

Poet Dog

Poet dog / sad dog
Fluffy / Ziggy / pink dog

Dream poet/sad poet
Dog. . .

      Ziggy and I alone in the woods

      Terri gone to Florida with her dog Puma
      to visit her mother

      Ziggy's head on Terri's pillow

      When I go to pet him
      He spreads his legs

Faith

Faith is convulsive. Sick & poetic
Ziggy wants to go outside. I want to hide

Away from the hustlers and politicians
The transactions of reckless schemers

Reductive artifacts
Contract services and child labor

30 million vote for their favorite
X Factor™ Singing Star

Only 800 sign a petition to free
The Tibetan Poet from his Chinese prison

"Is it you, the flame that burns in the middle of a storm?
Is it you, the boat that rocks in the sea?
Is it also you, who offers the torch of life in the darkness of night?"
- Tashi Rabten

"Don't waste your vote, vote for yourself!"

WOOF! WOOF!

*

Market Day
Book dealers in Lebanon

Rasheed in the spring
Shakespeare and call to prayers

In the UAE
Astronomy and creativity

Ptolemy's *Harmony*
Two graphic novelists in censored green of Arab Spring

"Until the bomb drops there are only nice speeches"

Murder in Tahrir Square

35% of the 99% supports the 99%

WOOF!

A clod of ghosts in the monastery of poetry
Stuck in the mud beyond the fiery zenith

Pillars of Adonis, Zarathustra and Hercules
Do-gooders enslaved at the arch

Wall St. bulls on a golden cable hung from a black hole

Philosophers and priests
Borrow light, spend darkness

Fictions full of ego and gluttony
Blue impact of a broken star

This Horder's Diversion
This simple wool spun from the beast

The World

I was alone in a world full of promise
But it couldn't keep its promise

Torn at the seam
Poetic in its primal form

The newsy diaphragm heaves
Under the weight of a bluesy cloud

Toxic Weiner Dog

A toxic wiener dog in the snow
So cute!

Do not whine, O puppy mine!
Be grand in freedom's addiction

Dog Animal
Dog named Peanuts

Three Dog Night
This fading perpendicular

Falling second
Captured in another gilded bone

Set upon this watery dark
What do you care for at all?

This mutation of light drains away
Light and dark confused by a second

Rank of premature vendors
Pink stamp collectors and rampant gloxinias

She insists on talking to me
While I'm trying to write poetry

About screaming children and dogs
She reads from the internet

About the airline industry's unfair treatment of Truffles
A corporate conspiracy against puppies

Truffles alone in the dark
Truffles after dark

A dog named Truffles

I wait for his bark and it never comes
Only peanuts, and peanuts come salted or unsalted in a bag

    *

Stewardship

How many of the 99% aspire to be the 1%?
Poetry suffers daily with the poet's imprisonment

Last Sunday afternoon at Jim's House
We hurry to hang on to what we can't let go of

Art is a gift, the gift a commodity
even if it's infatuated with itself

Ziggy sleeps

I've never been good at making money, or keeping money
But I've got good ideas & I care about people

    *

Occupy!

The Devil called the other day
Well not really the Devil but a poetry soldier

So used to fighting the Devil he's got Stockholm Syndrome
Only understands a top down authority

The blood on his clothes, his delicate fingers
Convinces him of this

He can't see that angel born of the terra firma
In ascension, holds the key to the kingdom of heaven

Ascension

Don't call me, I tell him, I've got nothing more to say to you
Until you understand

We share the vagrant's destiny

Ascension

Abrazos, yes, many *abrazos* and kisses too
But fair is fair, don't try to control each step

The greater good is self-determinant

How many of the 99% paid 30 dollars to see
Elizabeth Taylor's Diamonds?

How many of the 99% go to Rockefeller Center to see
The million dollar Christmas Tree?

My hands shake
My head shakes all the way down to my toes

I'm talking to myself when no one's looking
I begin with this word, "Listen!"

Talk myself into perspective
But there's no time for love

I tell myself, fair is fair, don't try to control
Each step, the greater good, is self-determinant

Then Ziggy cries for no human reason

I can't understand his dogged impatience
He doesn't understand indefinite detention…

Smart dog!
And where is Puma in this poodle diptych?

Two weeks ago he was at the vet
Because he lost a pound Terri couldn't find

Now he's in Hollywood, Florida with Terri
Eating large slabs of pizza

Happy Holidays, Puma, Ziggy, Terri!
I wish I could be there too.

So does Ziggy
It's so boring here in this drippy grove
We can't wait or count another cold second alone

Change is waiting for us everywhere
To get up and go! Bow wow! The future is now!

We don't need to develop an appropriate legal regime
We're free!

Moving With Terri

Moving, always moving
Rain and broken pine needles behind me

Spider on a rock by the window
Hawk crosses the treetops. Gone

Follow this
Follow that

Green barnacled bottle from Gulf of Mexico
Travels across United States in a box

In a moving truck to the Pacific coast
Lands on the shelf beside family photos

A gold eagle perched on a geode crystal
Driftwood, incense burner, mala

The prayers always happening and
A satchel for the ashes of the dead

Here come the ashes
Here come the dead.

Dancer

"Don't touch me"

A ballet of soldiers
Planted in a pastoral mindscape

"I am Nijinsky."

The Sewing Machine: The Perfect Art

The Sewing Machine, in Beirut, the Age of Iron
Still writing the same book, the story of war

The recurring taxi driver crossing the border
The square of martyrs, the relics
The core sample of horror

*

The literary stars

The celebrated journalists of the mind movie
The parade, this idyllic history

Was it our memory?
Was it our lives?

Or something we read somewhere?
In someone else's fairy tale?

A bridge between fictions?
A plot, an *Andalusian House*, an obsession?

How does one write about an era?

The misrepresentation of juxtapositional occasions
without belonging

The pride, the reinstated
The rejuvenated suburbs of ancient arts

The elegant repressions, the sun and sky

The peers. And peerless roses
on many walls of the deported
Muslims and Jews

Oh Granada!

*

The characters of Algeria
The picaresque resistance of secret languages

The code, the inner force of love
This is where the thread is broken

The weave worn by a tower of abrasions
The war in Afghanistan

*

This is where the dream fails
The lie is a predisposition

The precondition, the heritage
The fiction, contradiction, stupidity

The radicality without affinity
The ideology

The innocent, reluctant prophet of repression
The question of basic principles

The artificial existential constructs

The soot–heavy snow barracks
in the sacred cities born of blood

The tortured allegation
The stories never told

The panel of reductive inductees to the excoriated genre
Sets the ocean on fire, the nature betrayed

*

The oil, churches, mosques

The elderly, the heretics, the smoldering
The cigarette extinguished on the forehead of the asphyxiated nun

The tolerance deprived of bread and butter
The three daughters and the evolution of peace

We bless what no longer exists
The perfect art.

Ode to Tralfamadorian Goose

I am a Tralfamadorian, seeing all time as you might see a stretch of the Rocky Mountains. All time is all time. It does not change. It does not lend itself to warnings or explanations. It simply is. Take it moment by moment, and you will find that we are all, as I've said before, bugs in amber.

  Kurt Vonnegut, *Slaughter-House Five; or,*
  The Children's Crusade, a duty dance with death

Tralfamadorian Goose!

Global mother, lover, confidante in bubble, co-creator, wonder!
Gift, released from metal voice, iron clad guilt shackle, shrapnel of lost attachments

Chocolate beauty marks on velvet collarbone, and tangerine breast, blush
Spirit of red earth and air, tongue adoring in my ear drips honey bee, sweet care

Swinging hip dance, singing love's low trance, oh high sensation!
Golden eggs on blue moon pillows, transcendent willows coo in outer space

Forgiving fate, unfolding, luscious ripe and lotus great, iris true
Heart, where've you been, your swells of daylight ease through freeze of my cold life?

So different from caged bird, me, winged dream, beyond
Come tell me how we'll go on, you want to be stroked, I'm at your call, and on, and on

Goddess in cocoon, flesh-mate in caress, secret, soft in down
Transported, now, we can outlive, gently now, gentle you, and give, and how, just now

Tralfamadorian Goose!

Shy, robust fragrance of peach, woman, discrete plum lust
Gush of halo, resting indulgent in patter of me, flatter me, lather me in whispers

Steaming with purple borscht, piroshky, ambitious
Emotional, cautious, changeable, vulnerable council of playful, elegant pride

Tripping up bloody marching boots of muddy Red Army
Stinging keys with classical quotes, flushing out Satan disguised as hope, Cupid

Pecking Freud on forehead, waddling over therapy of rigor mortis
Shuttling a silver harp from heaven to heaven, gathering, weaving loose ends of life

Vonnegut understood this time, and you would understand it too
Basking in gardens, listless moments, ready to leap upon inspiration, waiting

No single man's invention, Bacchanalia, Rubens, the feast is named
Picnic, banquet, treasure of favorite desire, unquenchable, hungering, basket of spice

I never trusted women, until she came along, now there's only you
(She wrecked her car on the freeway, screamed hysterical, mourning a point already moot)

Tralfamadorian Goose!

Following you, following me, in a good old fashioned stand-off
Face to face, shouldering obligation, holstering family, how will it turn out, who knows?

Watching guards change into loons at Lenin's tomb, May Day
KGB refuse swan egg pastries, Intourist room above staggering stream of banners

White feather quills dipped in solvent of defection, migration
Bodies daily turning up in newspaper pages, history recovering in revelation

Jews and Russians, holes in their chests as big as *War and Peace*
Infected caverns stuffed with poetry, longing, vodka, roses, icons, fish, horseradish

Making love in secrecy, discovery, uncovering a moist lyrical fetish
Cuddles, wriggles, moans, invisible tundras of memory, raves, a Siberian diplomacy

Giggles, baby talk, pinches, digging nails in buttocks, chirps, sleep
Dream I'm someone else, when I awake, holding you, you're in someone else's dream

Tralfamadorian Goose!

Chagall, Poe, Eartha Kitt, Isadora Duncan compose your choir
Painting Matrushkas of Iago, Zhivago, Lolita, Jesus, and Yeltsin's quadruple heart bypass

Looking lost, forever homeward, swearing intimacy, constant truth
Vow your love, won't take it back, love transient as democracy in real fists of greed

Tossing stone baggage overboard so body, spirit, floats, arise!
Fly with radio on, cigarette, rouge-chic, bearing down on pedal of empire's success

Rushing about, picking caress off gossip, pitch of neighbor's fence
Building fire storm with hug and smile, destruction calling me close, no more than I do

Tralfamadorian Goose!

Bigger than me, the oyster is yours, blue pearl of your eyes
Cherish me, render me, naked in gold-black boundless flesh of this starry night

There's no one else for me, and you, but you so smooth
Fidelity comes in confession of infidelity, addiction in rejection of past, goodnight

Conclude the paragraph, the verse, the breath, you knew that if
Being here was an experiment the ideal would always remain fiction, that's right!

This, from an imperfect world, tired of suspicion, you still want him too
Promises, only couplets, spoken in a sinking craft, so when at last, I'm gone, I'm gone.

Groggy

War and missing weapons
Weapons and missing limbs
News and missing ballots
Democracy and missing

Terri,

missing democracy, both of us

Far away.

Poem For Mitko

Today, when Ziggy
(the dog) and I
go down to the ocean
we'll send you a poem

Some wild ribbon
invisible soul
birds in flight
across chrome waters

We will wait
for your silent reply
Look for a word
And world of peace

Riding back
over bright breakers
From your land-
locked European country

*

A Sea-Monkey
I was born and raised
in Florida

Learned my liquid life
Now, I am pulled
by the moon

Birth and inevitability
Yes, the ocean
Gives us power

Tells us the rolling universe
Does not belong to us
No matter how hard

We try to destroy it

*

Godless power
Chrome waves

Sun's flames
soak my brow

Ziggy stops to dig in the sand
Barks at the blue-black raven

Calling from the stranded
Boulder on Shell Beach

    *

I'd go crazy living on an island
Surrounded by a fevered sea of woe

And sapphire horizons

I plan for a busier tomorrow
But I can't get the ocean out of my head

You could crave another island

But whatever's there I can't describe
Lupine, thistle, and wild oats

On the bluff
Something I think I see, but can't

Imagination
Inscribed in the mercurial sky

I wait for an explosion

*

This is not a good year for Tyrants
Copper skies above Tahrir Square

Here comes that crashing thought
That currency I sent away over the expanse

To be read by you, Mitko
Tear gas clouds in Tahrir Square

Coming back tied and frayed around a rugged headland
We have had enough of this enslavement!

Men and women, boys and girls with stones
Give them what they want

Don't wait for permission from the headquarters
Authorization from the Opera

Live long and without endorsements

*

The dog still barks, but can't say exactly what he believes
Is that a dragon or civilization burning on the beach?

Coming in or going out
I can't tell which way the poetry is running

A wave followed by another wave followed by another
A sleeper wave

Tide of the underworld rushing overall, blowing silver
Over shipwrecked shores and tortured skies

*

I asked the California badger
on the road back home
Do you find this dream amusing?

There was something vicious in his response
Is the human condition just entertainment?

I ask the badger
about Political gamesmanship
and coppery metaphors

Slung across the heavens
like Handel's Messiah?

No reply!

This is not a domestic animal!

*

O, Brother from another great continent
Beyond shimmering cataclysmic fever

Foam and light rushing up over my feet
Mammoth rubbings on mammoth stones. . .

Oh Macedonian Brother

I went down to the ocean today and the sky and sun and water
were blinding and gorgeous chrome, so I kind of got caught

in light and isolation and could think of nothing else.

3

Head Shed

1.

Legacy for sale at End Times
Resurrection bodies on loan

        Tribulation, divination, dispensation
        Split the moon

Form is the rage

It's too late for redemption
Blue jays murder finches like madmen in Iraq

Heat waves flood and submerge the Nation

The whole green planet drips
A musical dichotomy of poles going extinct

2.

Chimney blows blue smoke
Fat creek booms
Wholly terrified sleep

Conflict diamonds
Smuggled through the night

James Brown lies in state
At the Apollo Theater
Peace demands a public hanging

                    BOOM!

Here comes the garbage truck
Media trash bagged for universal incineration
Sunrise Sanitation bills every second Monday
Of every Second Coming

"This Year At War continues. . ."
God kills!

Rhododendron leaves curl in the freeze
Ice crunchy mud
Hell frozen over
Chile rellenos keep me warm

3.

I cut a full moon out of a photo
Paste it beside a Möbius Strip
Capture a language

Bury my head in my hands
A white book sails through the sky

I read creek melodies
From the future
I grow bald before I turn gray

4.

Mailquake
Stressbox
Palindrome

Shun, shun, shun

    Miss Manners
    Co-opts
    For Calvinism

    Polite Liberalism about
    WAR

        Fro-Zen

See silent protest
See boycott

A monk returns from the ashes and sets the record straight
Bells ring in Katmandu!

*

Iraqi babies dead
Bombed Lebanese dead
Turn to the "Turning Wheel"
For instructions on how to act and feel

*

I found a baby crying in the street
    Occasionally they wander out alone, these kids

    Whatever...

Saturday in August
Slaughter continues
Gnaw, gnaw, yes

    Three coffees and a dry bowl of cereal

5.

Some nights I can't sleep
Or scream

Splash of red leaves
Clutters the driveway

Rain everywhere
But the creek is dry

Jazz tells me what to think
Hardball plays hardball

6.

Birth pains of Venus

Uranium Desert Anarchy

Bowls   Seals   Trumpets

Oh, Mad Monk of Ephemeral Embalmment!

        Rapture Index: Moderate to Heavy prophetic activity

Gorgonzola & walnut ravioli from Michael McClure

"Invasion of the Thunderbolt Pagoda" from Ira Cohen
Sundance with Jampa Dorje

                (The) energy goes to Heaven

7.

White chickens beside a pearly gate

8.

          To document my own death & art

Brad and Angelina, Cézanne

            Afraid of every minute

"You have a cold, that's all. You're not dying!"
I am dying, any second now. . .

A banyan tree falls through the roof
Volcano explodes in Indonesia

Shoe bomber kills ten in Baghdad mosque

Writing with devotion
To transform existence

A woman's head rolls
Out of the cab of her husband's truck

Paul McCartney's birthday falls
On Sunday, "Yesterday"

A previously unknown letter
Written by Mary Shelley is discovered
At an antiques fair in Tuscany, Italy

I follow ashes that eventually disappear
Death comes too close
So I write myself to sleep

9.

I walk the dog down the country road
He pants, old and tumorous: still tugs at the leash

Ripe blackberries in a thorny tangle 'round
The mail box. Lilies scorched

Almost lunchtime, getting hungrier
The dog thinks all Art is futile

10.

Spontaneous Expurgation
Doodles & Sketches

        All in Time will Heal
        Vanishing Windows

Cloudy Eyes
Slide on Copper Wire

        Between Wisdom and Obedience

Smokestacks & Refineries
Raw Tongue on Rough Teeth

            Splashing Firestorm

11.

        "Break the cross, spill the wine"

            Ice on the car and sky electric

12.

I don't want to see the end of the world
But somebody has already written a soundtrack

13.

EPIGENESIS ON TEMPLE MOUNT

Titulus:

Bobblehead Bisrima "Très Riches Heures du Duc de Berry" Oracle of Mt. Hula Hula Buried in white shrouds for stoning Second Coming of Stayaway Saint

Brocken spectre Walpurgisnacht

Golden-armed Soldiers of Moral Liberation Bonfire of Darwinian acolytes Jihadist Cremated for *delatio domini*. Magic birth quantum entanglement

Repent!

Matthew 25:13

Luke 21:36

I Peter 3:9

I Timothy 6:14

Titus 2:13

Repent!

Inflationary speculative wailing Celestial fire Blood sacrifice in dream time Zodiac Kabobs of Humanist Silverfish Nuclear Calendars of Talmudic Salvation Midnight Cyclone of dragon horn and ash Heavenly mountaintops tremble Under Esdras Paul and Saint Perpetua shawled in smoke and semen Mohammed and Sibylline hooves Songs of Sodomizing rams and glory!

    "*Agere dare ferre* or *tollere in crucem*"

Gloom of oil engorged shit clouds of fear Skoll devours the sun His brother Hati eats the Moon Unholy retribution Legislated ecstasy Pandemic influenza

    Dysautonomic

Night shakes Subterfuge of franchised

    Glossolalia

Monopoly Bondage Justice and Horror Strikes Invasions Vagrancy and Plague Insurgencies of the veil

    Shugyo

Hathor

Krishna

Vishnu

Maitreya

Buddha

Slayer

Cannibal Corpse

Sepultura

Agere dare ferre or *tollere in crucem*

Flagellations of False Prophets Fixed Dice of Zoroaster Hoodlum Texas Presidents Imams of Atlantis and New Zion Clairvoyant Kings of East and West 10:50am September 16 Poppies smuggled in bowels of toy whales Biblical prophylactics Elysian Fields Injected in rotted veins of terminal Idealists Wind up crackhead dolls Disney Bunker Buster puppets Video Sanhedrin Mules of Apostasy Mark of the Beast Supernatural moral quacks Dogmas and Decrees Hysteria Celebratory disunity Universal Planetary gangrene God Democracy Theocracy Reed Fields Prick Screw bolt Witches Brew

Arbor infelix

Circumambulation

L Arbre du Ténéré

Churches robberies slander prophetic impersonations Mediocrity Temples of Persia Israel and Gog Tonatiuh the Rising Eagle Council of Steroid Magicians

Gotterdammerung

Pole shift

Earth change

Cosmic convergence

    Hajj...

"Take ye heed, watch and pray: for ye know not when the time is."

4

The Book

1

Grappling hook.
Telephone.
Unpleasant dreams I was turning about.
Bookshelf.
Meat rack.
Rearranging my mind like a bookshelf.

"That's a project."

My projects.
Books I have to read to finish what I've set out to do.
Buy a tape transcription device. (Batteries and typist not included).
This chair.
Right here.
Isn't high enough to reach the keyboard.
Or play out the melody of addiction.
That small hand drum.
Fish drum played with all kinds of Buddhist prayers.
Buddhist drum, prayer drum.
All kinds of drums.

"You've been picking up a lot of stray dogs lately.

Maybe you should do something for yourself."
There were things she could do that no one else should do.

"I think we're breaking up here."

All systems gone.
Those newspaper clippings of community activities. Go!
My activities. Clippings. Headed for the scrapbook. Scrap heap.
Laws and promises to snakes and frogs that must be kept.
Our green world is melting.

Melting cap.
Swarming flies.
Snow seals boil.
Look out the window.
A dead horse.
One Beat.
One family life.
Dead.

"The ultimate consequence."

The Traveling Mind.
Get up, go out. Drive a while. See what's out there. Talk to a stranger.
Wear something you wouldn't ordinarily be caught dead wearing.
No underwear.
Living with the dead.

"Watch where you're going!"

Walking with The Living Dead.
Through "Sublime Fudge."

2

Scrumptious without nutritional value. Super-rational with cherries on top.
Divine works of art.
At Dairy Freeze. Dairy Queen. Smother all flavors with toppings, hazelnut, raspberry sauce, marshmallow sauce, crushed walnuts, peanut butter slabs, chocolate sprinkles, cookie crumbs, sublime fudge.
With cherries on top.
Smothering literary criticism, smothering . . .
Why can't I just say I do it because I want to? Because it feels good?

Sublime Fudge.
Something to hang your hat on.
You need something gross. Gross profit.
Out of one of those stuffy books by stuffy critics on stuffy books by stuffy critics on stuffy books. Read them you might learn something.
Stuffing myself.
Folding socks. Tying up loose ends.

Sublime Fudge.
You can't live on that. Leaves you empty, craving.
Assay the literary landscape. Excavate and mitigate. Sublimate and divinate. Tenure. Tenant farmer. Sharecropper. Slave to sublime fudge.

"Divine. Simply divine."

Divinating fine words in a blank book thick as *War & Peace*. On a book shelf. Blank books of lost and illuminated hours. Illuminated books of lost words and extinct flowers on precious vellum and gold leaf.
A plaster cast of William Burrough's fist and ass.
Serving up the grand reception. Silver and linen. Many forks of many sizes. Deception.

One for grapefruit. Many spoons. One for scouring the inside of Easter eggs.
For serving up the resurrected fetus of Jesus, legs pinned to a wishbone.
The main course of funeral vulture and a three year back-log of stinking corpse flesh.

"It was a perfect day for a picnic but we ate inside."

3

Party favors and games followed the ringing of the tingling of the bells.
Cat-of-nine tails and Pin The Tail On The Donkey. Hurrah!
A stack of soiled napkins and lamb bones on bone china.
We pushed back our chairs. Away from the table. We were up for it.
Blind-folded, we marched past soldiers from the Army of the Living Dead
into The Mylar Chamber where we were filmed at play by a mute ventriloquist speaking through the lips of a stuffed red velvet-legged frog slumped on a faux Formica pedestal.
The photographer with pouty lips, and a smoke-singed eye for prepubescent girls wheezed as he focused on our reflections, joked through his gray, brittle beard, to break the ice, then spoke slowly.

"Smile!"

What a sight we were and how we held our breath and smiled.
Held our breath then laughed.
Swinging like a bird in an iron cage at the town square. Jailbird. James Dean.
Pickled herring. Gregory Corso.
Everywhere about the country celebrations to honor Creation.
Nobel Laureate for Gene Splicing. Cloning.
No one knows who was actually taking the pictures or whether they would turn out good.
But there was a walrus of contact sheets mounting and copulating as the virtuoso ventriloquist valedictorian violinist with micro-macro lens snapped off ten hundred rolls of film.
Then we died of laughter.
The post-operative party now in full swing.
Going.
That's when the sores began to erupt on my gums.

    "Stigmata."

Silver nitrate applied to small sores.
The wound finally cauterized.

    4

Bow down. You are about to partake in the . . . What have you got against . . .
Arriving by mail . . .
Submissions.

    "Excuse me while I close the door."

Art and Poetry.

    "Don't let that shit in. It will foul the air."

Too late, my lovely, too late.

    "Lovely."

Stories and letters.
From strangers sent—
Because I have an organ, appendage, signage, appreciation, a champion of the lettered grunt and groan. A uterine wall where the egg can attach and prosper. Seeds can germinate. Sprout four legs and mouth. Propagate.
Letters from strangers, stories and letters sent for deposit because I have a bank. Bank book for issuing checks. Accountable. Deposit slips. Five years of boxes dating back five years, for the IRS.
To make a gold mine of inspiration.
To make a reward for sincere efforts.

    "He tries . . ."

That's what Gregory Corso said when asked what he thought of Allen Ginsberg's poetry:

    "Allen?" he said, "He tries."

I heard it second-hand from Ira Cohen.

Deposit inspiration in caverns of hollow-boned and ephemeral wings.
That's what they send them here for.

Off you go now. Off to school. Learn and follow the golden rule.
Out the door. Fly the coop.
The body wastes. Wanes in a hospital bed wearing a tiara of rock stars and poetry legends. A self-confessed "commie dope fiend."

"Where was I?"

Gregory Corso is dying. From cancer.

"Yes, I know that. But where was I?"

You shouldn't have to ask . . .

5

AFTERTHOUGHTS FROM THE AFTERWORLD

"Great name for a book."

I don't get it. What's it about?
Death. Metaphysics. Voice. Breath. Metaphysics. Death.
You shouldn't have to ask.

"You want an apology?"

That would be in order.

"As you wish."

Death is the ultimate consequence.
The Traveling Mind encounters Sublime Fudge which is overblown literary criticism.
French theorists and Russian doctors deliver babies in swimming pools somehow reducing the trauma of moving a fish to land.
Derrida. Barthes.
Deconstruction.
Little green apples grafted on a tomato vine.

    "Just make sure you put it back right, when you put it back."

Sublime fudge.
Genetically engineered inspiration.
Hand growing out of middle eye so it's not so much what you see
but what you can get
a hold of.

    "Fudge."

To fake it.
The voluminous manifestations of unsettled mind, a family carcass. Cotton erupting from hornless skull of a white rhino. Black rhino.
Some kind of fluff.
Sublime fudge. Kill for it.

    "Poached."

Speak clearly into the tape.

    "That's what I'm doing."

You're being recorded.

"I am?"

Yes, you're being recorded for prosperity, posterity, posterior ruminations.
Chapters in a book.
The title of the book is?

"The Book."

Where does it begin?

"Anywhere you like."

I've been told this is the way to begin. To go about it. Another thing to go about.

6

AFTERTHOUGHTS FROM THE AFTERWORLD

Afterworlds.
Sunlit tree trunks on pine needle slopes. Brown tufts of needles among green tufts
of needles on tufts of branches on saplings and giant kings of the mountains and queens
of the latitudes among tufts of lime green lichens on brittle groping tufts of dead wood.
Tired of synthesis. In a colony. A windbreak.
Deaths.
Habitations.
Small and large breaths. *Exultations* and *Personae*. Exhalations

and masques. Barbarians in sophisticated horn rimmed octagonal warrior helmets with matching coat of mail adorned with watery diadems. Ruby diadems.
Sophisticated love positions.
Habitations.
Shelters from the storm. Hatched ruts. Thatched, Scotch-taped hay bale huts planted out in the flood plain.
Coming from. A world we imagine.
It could be a stage with a chair. A tiny table. A ringworm. Hair on a nest of "smashed potatoes." (Thank you, PW).
A cough off stage. A rehearsal. Or full dress performance.
Pantomime. A place where people go to be entertained.
Or get paid very little to perform.

7

Here we are again. Right here again. This desk of paper and pens. Afterthoughts from the Afterworld.

"Sublime Fudge."

It's obvious. The effort to clarify only makes the sky cloudier.

"Why the sky?"

Because it's a lofty choice in the groveling heap of stink and piss.
The telephone rings.

"Answer it! It might be the King. Someone important. The President."

No, I don't think so. I've already heard from all the really important people. And they're dead.

> "Do you truly believe that? Are you that cynical?"

I'm not cynical. I'm an idealist. Anti-Utopian Idealist.

> "I don't get it."

Here's the missing heart. I found it dying in the bloodless highway of postures and postulations, promotions and gimmicks, almost a stone, almost crumbling in my hand. Define the moment.
I know it's the heart. There's no other heart. The last one came to a screeching halt in a laboratory at Disney Land. The autopsy concluded:

> "The imagination is not the heart. It's not going to go anywhere."

Referring to what?

> "The heart. It's not going to run away. Put it down and let me have a look see."

But it seems important that…

> "Don't worry. If there isn't something to worry about, you'll find something to worry about."

You make me angry. That worries me.

> "That is not a relic. You are so dramatic!"

That's my job. This is my heart. Go away. You're killing me. You're making me die.

    "I am very tired. That's up to you. I have to sleep now. We can talk about this tomorrow. I'll call you tomorrow after work. It will be very late."

8

The book of poems by the dying man.
The book of poems by the sublime poetess in her constant pursuit of a mythology.
Pens in red. Pens in black. Pencils that erase their own mistakes.
Indelible impressions.
I can't resist the hot coffee in the blue Chinese ceramic mug.

    "No wonder your arms hurt. You are always writing and never resisting."

I'm not writing anymore. I'm witnessing. Being sensitive. A surgeon from Nepal has come to install a Senso-Meter behind my sternum. It's a routine operation but painful. There are drugs involved. A perk.

    "It's not so much the pain of the surgery, but the recovery that tries one's soul. Why do you allow this?"

What else am I to do? I don't have the money to find true love or buy it. And I don't have the courage to join the brave new world or leave it alone.

    "Another poetic manifestation."

Another clawing at bliss to be more precise. You didn't even ask.

> "Let me know when you're fully recovered. Meanwhile, can I get you anything at the store?"

I can't resist hot coffee or the medicine cabinet.
The triangular blue pills in the medicine bottle.
Bran muffins. Diet soda. Chunk white tuna. Low fat chocolate cookies.

> "I'm back!"

Staring at the door. There's a sign on the inside: "Leave this man in peace."
I won't go through that door for fear of disturbing this man.

> "Are you feeling better?"

Thanks for asking.
Did you get me comic books? Or a copy of Penthouse. I like to look at the pictures.

But she forgot the heart tucked under her arm. And we were fresh out of tissue paper. What was the point?

> "The Senso-Meter. Does it work?"

The Senso-Meter makes me incapable of self-annihilation.
(Who is speaking here?)

I make my bed. Hang up my jacket. Turn down the heater. Put away my robe.
I'm always cold unless the sun burns through the outer layer of flesh which is only appearances.

Unless the sun burns through the sternum and boils the blood around the Senso-Meter.
But the Senso-Meter is misfiring at this very moment. Right here.
Because the blood is boiling but there's no sign of a wobbling arrow.
The heart, the last heart, the final winged heart with horns and a walking stick, may not, will not survive, I'm sure of it. Revive.

"You better come up with a plan quick or else you'll die."

Surely.
(Who is speaking here?)
Didn't you read the sign on the door.

"Leave this man in peace."

9

LIVING WITH THE WALKING DEAD

Battery packs. Rechargeable batteries. Transformers.
I'm going to go outside and sit in the sun for a while.
Away from the telephone and great literature.
Garbage cans.
I'm getting up and going outside with the dog. The Dog!
Ahh, Traveling Mind.
Operating manuals. Calendars.

August 26, 2000: Cordless Integrating Answering Device with Caller ID.

"Is that you?"

Stereophonic devices that muffle the music playing in the mind. That plays in a remembered mind.

I want this Senso-Meter. But it's a foreign object. It functions like success at the bottom of a well. Like road-kill on a banquet table. Possum on a toothpick. Skunk walking on the lips of a dainty psychiatrist, legs crossed around the possibility of a Manhattan skyscraper.

"What are you waiting for? Why don't you go outside and sit in the garden? Or go down to the beach and let the ocean blow through you?"

I'm just about to do that. Take a shower and drink from the probable cause . . .
But first I must save everything.

10

Begin with The Book.

"I was just about to do that."

Poems dedicated to Gregory Corso coming in the mail. Gregory dying from cancer. Hermes is Gregory. Gregory is Nuncio. Tumorous wings on his leather shoes.

"Unruly magic in his hollow bones."

Poems fly from New York to San Francisco. In light of fading powers.
Sublime, eternal powers.
Gregory's fate is not tied to the postal service. The messenger is not working for the government. The messenger is a magician with other ways of working. Though nothing should be ruled out when magic is put to purpose.

    "Or not."

Exactly.

    11

THE LIVING DEAD

Walking with the living dead.

"Hi," I said. Waving my hands across their glazed gazes, the undead, dead haze.
I'm sure they were aware of it, but had something else on their mind.
Weighing them down. Preoccupied.
Living with the dead. Walking on the moon. Bumper cars on Mars.

Wake up and smell the roses. The plastic pinwheels that smell like hoses in a suburban summer.
Sprinklers play church music.
A sad commentary on physics.
The flight of stones, agate, and molecular bits and pieces threatening to blow up this world. Unless we map it quick.
Mars and the living dead.
Cigars from pre-revolution Cuba smoking from his head. He spits in the street and looks

uphill as the trolley rolls back down and crushes his alligator shoes. Another species lost. Map those meteorites and comets quick or we're done for, any day eventually, and inevitably. Make laser guns and pinpoint razor bombs to annihilate small buildings headed our way.
Better do it now. Map it!

12

He "lives with a clam in a shell."
No wonder there's no time for pure thoughts or an empty mind.
The dictionary. Fat and red. It doesn't know everything. But ponders and lumbers.
No wonder there's no time for silent contemplation and complacent blindness without near death experience from sexual exhaustion.
Mars. Meteorites.
Lamps.
Heavenly orbs.
Sometimes brighter than the sky.
Lamps.
Right here on the desk.
An old address book that has lost its front page and numbers to the weariness of calling out. When nothing else seemed to matter.
A new address book purchased in a moment of renewed hope. Not enough numbers yet to be everything, but more than the old dog-eared address book.

It's still becoming.
The Traveling Mind.
Traveling over the face of things. The fabric of phenomena. Shoelaces. Weary carpet. Right here beneath my slippers.

New slippers lined with wool. Reliable leather soles on reliable feet that have become reliably sensitive. I know they're sensitive because I wear these feet regularly.
To that I speak.
Of sensitive feet.
Of plugs to printers, scanners, tendons that spasm to shadowy output of unquestionable genius.

    "Now that we have that settled . . ."

If you don't believe me you ought to get a new hairdresser.

    "I did."

Just don't cut it. It looks better long.

    "But it gets in my face. My hair is heavy. It gives me a headache."

Getting back to the moment.
Carpal tunnel syndrome. Impingent tendonitis— shoulders. Looking in my wallet for the diagnosis. For the remedy. Prescription for physical therapy two times a week for a month. Laced with Vicodin.
Pharmaceutical solutions are often the best solutions.

13

A weak bladder. I go back into my files. /August 12, 2000: "If I hurt someone/ Afraid of myself/Reading a book/Writing/ A can of worms/Condom."

BOOK (in four chapters).

1) The Traveling Mind.
2) Living with the Dead.
3) Afterthoughts from The Afterworld.
4) "Sublime Fudge."

Afterthoughts from the Afterworld like double jeopardy.
Go backwards then forward, filling it in.
Unless there's another where to go. Another place of purpose. A beyond afterworld.
A world to go on living with the walking dead.
There must be another world.

14

"Here I am."

I knew you would be, sooner or later.

"And the afterworld?"

It's a real dream, I swear! I didn't make it up.

"What does it look like?"

Sit down. It will be right here.

    15

Drive-Thru Absolution. Drive-Thru Limbo. Drive-Thru Reconciliation…
    Another idea to calcify the heart. Run cholesterol and aggression through the bloodstream.

    "You're morbid."

Not really. It's just that the circus is adding rings. Three rings. Nine rings.
A twelve ring circus. Hell!
Kaleidoscopic lightwaves under the Very Big Top.

    "You're cruel."

I'm not intentionally cruel. Something poisonous moves through me. Infiltrates.
A blind fury escapes my mouth.
Dry mouth. Singing gums and lips.
A scream passes through my torso into the tree limbs until it finds the browning leaves, red and orange-gold leaves. My probing fingers.
I try to stop the bile. It's a mind working on its own, a virus from a genetic mutation, an instruction from another afterworld inflames the tendons in my shoulders.
My fingers whisper kindness because I was taught to be good.
Isn't that enough! Isn't that enough suffering and imagination!

    "Question or exclamation?"

Bliss dome. Dustbin.

Gloom home.
Hell hole. Slop bowl.

The other side of here where things can be considered.

Gold light. Blue light.
Measure the intensity.
The Vicodin kicks in.

Black arrow on Senso-Meter spins wildly, searches for an Alfred Hitchcock movie. Ghost figures writhe in yellow smoke light . . . drowning the government official, the general and the author of Sublime Fudge.

    16

"Sublime Fudge."

Chapter 16.
It isn't easy to teach a gorilla eating manners. It's easier to teach a chimp.

    "But the dog comes back when I call. Most of the time."

Screaming at the heat.
In a heat.
Blow on it.
Blow on that spoon of chowder.
Those tender lips. That small tongue split at the road not taken, flashing back into horror.
. . . regretting.

The dead are incapable of regret.
Or memory.
While others walk in the mire of Sublime Fudge.
Open or closed.
Transparent.
Opaque.
I want to feel good about myself without feeling horny.
I'm taking control.

Afterthoughts. Trolling off the back of a boat in a junkyard of dreams.

    "Who is steering?"

Through this Sublime Fudge.
The propeller turns, the line runs out, rod tip bends against the drag of dusk.

    "Who is steering?"

I am.

    "Where to?"

Why ask, isn't it enough you get to go fishing? Now sit up in your chair and take a deep breath and be grateful that any moment chance or serendipity may yield a glorious manifestation.

    "Like what?"

Six wings on a drill bit articulated bodiform sweating honey in moonblue radiance. Eyes approximately six feet from the rotating form wavering ganglion with synaptical aptitude emitting a whale-like song with bat-like intuition at frequencies only a Labrador retriever can hear when it has a mind to.

"So where's the practical component?"

If you were interested in money you should never have gotten involved with a poet.

17

SUB CHAPTER: APPARATUS:

My personal forest.
On the other side of the window.
This side.
Flashcard. Storyboard.
Day long. Night long.
Sunny day. Foggy day.
Half sunny, half foggy day.
Inside or out. One way or another.
Puppets. Stick figures.

Long day inside or out.
One way or another.

"Are you feeling better?"

I always feel better when I'm not thinking about feeling.
But now that you remind me my fucking arm is killing me.

"Poor baby."

Long side. Outside.
Day puppets. Night figures.
Night sticks. Day trips.
Apparatus. Money.
Apparatus. Apple sauce.
Apparatus. Parachute.
Apparatus. Hat rack.
The Afterthought. The Sublime Fudge.
Living with the dead. Walking around the imagination.
The Traveling Mind.

"Don't forget about me."

You?

"Yes."

There's someone I must call.

18

BOOK I

[fill in here]

Slow down

19

THE TRAVELING MIND

[fill in here]

Even slower.

20

"Okay, I'll find the records. I didn't throw them out. I'm sure I put them somewhere."

Yes, you find the records. I'll put them together.

There's a job I have to complete that doesn't interest me anymore.
Tapes. Cassette tapes. Interviews.

"And humanity."

Afterthoughts from the Afterworld for the Afterworld.

I'm almost there.

"I'm going to work."

An untimely occupation.
Someone should underwrite the underground

      "When are you going to write another novel?"

There will be no other novel.

I love my job. It's what I've been telling myself for years.

Now, I have a mind to change my mind.

5

Track

Roots travel
Madrid to Galicia
Paris to bougainvillea

Field guide to love and civilization

Water the garden
War blossoms

Beauty and perpetual anxiety

Soul fire, sulfur, sullen harmonies

Solitaire
Out of the center

        *

Drunk at 2am
I knocked on Lennie's window
Woke him up
After an hour rambling on & on
He threw me out
The police picked me up on the street

Booked me for public drunkenness
and disturbing the peace

      *

Fan turns
105 degrees Fahrenheit outside
The dog licks his balls
I chew gum

      Bees swarm the baklava

      *

Peaches, plums, nectarines
Apricots and melons

      Barbecue three times this week
      Food is the only thing that interests me

Stiff ass and a bum gut
This might be a good time to get a real job

      *

Some beautiful puzzles broken and unfixable
It takes forever to hear back from the manufacturer

The dog poops on the end of a leash
Then pulls me down the road

The reference remains obscure

50 years towing the hoe, whoring the woe
And a handful of maple leaves shudder

Shift. Switch
Drop back or step in

I compose by contrast and condition

*

Slumber party in Orense

Raccoon knocks over birdbath
and crushes the abutilon

Looking for lots of places

Lizards chase each other
across the crunchy madrone leaves

On the death of Billy Graham's wife Ruth,
"a spiritual stalwart and modest mentor
who provided a solid foundation –
both biblically and geographically –
for her globe-trotting husband."

Billy tells the reporter,
"I wish you could look in that casket
because she's so beautiful."

I think I'll pass

      *

Corrosive devotion sweeps the theater

Leaky hot tub too hot to handle

Robert Johnson morning glory hat trick blues

      33 pounds of *noir* travel wear

Angel food cake itinerary

      Everything is depressed
      and second-rate

      *

A boy is lost in the redwoods
We look for him

      *

Invisible repair

*

Alone in the house
The hot tub too hot
I take a shower

*

Right here beside the rug is a house

What do I think of when I grind my teeth?
Everything!

Last night I read a poem by Miguel de Unamuno
Poet and philosopher born in Bilbao
who worked to dissolve the boundaries
between genres

Beauty resists resistance

*

Methhead whore
tricking truckers
on River Road

The World's Ugliest Politician
announced in New Jersey

                    *
Sleep without remorse

                *

Sudden oak death threatens the neighborhood

Spiders, mosquitoes, hip-hop, jazz
Anti-social dissociation and assemblage

                *

Yesterday's leaky toilet turned jackhammer
(some kind of air pocket in the pipes)...
How much will that cost?

Hernia surgery gone awry

Dog needs his teeth cleaned
Trunk release won't release

The surgeon says give it another 3 months
Meanwhile the blue jay tears up the garden

              *

"The door's wide open!" Terri says
            "I did it on purpose" I say
"I know but you're letting in all the bugs."

*

"Rich fucks."

*

Too full to shower
Too dirty to get into bed

Remember what the Buddha says:

"Stay Spunky!"

*

A man left a million dollar violin on a train

Another man got temporal mandibular joint malfunction
After shooting a man in the head while hunting grouse

*

You try, you try, you win, you fail

*

Drive across Pyrenees in an amphitheater

What is going on? I said to myself

*

EXTENDED METAPHOR
STRETCH THAT!

*

Mutual aid survives mutual funds
Utilities are over utilized
Craft kisses Art goodbye

*

6 squirrels lounge around the birdbath
Grooming, dozing, chirping

Rodents armed with knives
Try to kill me in my sleep

I make plans for revenge
They'll never catch me now!

*

I learn how to raise bees
Plant lemons in a wine barrel
Journalize delusion

*

A swarm of black bugs eat the house
Then attack the dog
I beat them back with a broom

A peacock comes to live on the deck
Beware of this feathered woman
she will possess you

Ruddy ferns on Goat Rock

*

My problem is that I want attention
But when I get it, it makes me nervous

. . .continuing

Spider silk stretches
from Morning-Glory
to glowing redwood

*

Arabs in Spain
Gypsies in Paris
Jews in America

Diaspora clothesline

"We are in a global state of emergency and must stabilize
our existence?" George Bush says

My son sits up until 3am watching movies about Spain
thinking about where he can buy a beer and a joint
with fake ID manufactured in Mexico

There would be no peace
even if we closed the borders.

We don't believe in peace
We believe in Original Sin.

        *

Shredded clouds
hover over the anxious house

        *

Reserve a room in Figueres

"A foot that is injured has no eyes,"
West Indian saying

        *

Castles, cider, Spain
Another fascist cemetery

Medieval romance
Next week Gaudi, octopus, tapas in general

Then to Paris

*

Bladder report
Short and urgent

Death over semantics

*

I don't need traveler's checks
I need a piggy bank for loose change
and a brain for loose screws

I'm not going into town today

Intervals
I found them in a file cabinet

A century ago
Yesterday, this morning, a minute ago

I am embraced by a shadow

*

Empty the hot tub
Move plants off the deck
Closer to departure

*

BUD POWELL IN BARCELONA

Rain all day & Joan Miró sleeps late
How many discos?
Bowls of fried minnows and olives
On the Ramblas
Go on some side street
Suddenly, Christ
There's a huge church that drips tears
and a mission of bells clang
Rome in ecstasy
Catalonia is not Spain
Marilyn Monroe in the "Metropolis"
You can see Paris Hilton everywhere
I remember The Surrealists

Nostalgic groves
A thousand cars bumper to bumper
Eager to visit that quaint little village, Cadaqués
Animal crackers in my *paella*
Take a picture
Ride back over the mountain

Cafe Americano
The singer is a fraud
VISPO is a village in Spain
"M" is for Maria Madrid
Aquarius, the world is your oyster
The earth is your old mother
Your sunglasses at home
Visions of *langostinos* on the promenade
The crooked line
The escalator
Gondola, Taxi *con gas*
Hernia on tranquilizer
Ascent of Miró
I had a print of one of his paintings
On my wall for 40 years
Tapestry!
Assassination of umbrellas

*

GAUDI BARCELONA TICKETS

25 Euro   Sagrada Família
16 Euro- Casa Batlló
16 Euro- La Pedrera

*

The Imagination of Space

*

We are so proud it kills us

*

Simplicity of paying bills
Complexity of dreaming

Terror of invention
Fear of insomnia

Donuts and boobs on the Costa Brava
Cured ham and clams

Outside Teatro Museo Salvador Dalí
Vertigo and a drunk art student from Denver

*

Salmonella

I can see the Eiffel Tower
from the toilet in my Paris hospital room

*

Deck builder hammers echo in redwood valley 8am
Art and prophecy a parlor trick

Chunks of sunburned Styrofoam become stelae
Illuminate a personal mythology

*

Déjà vu Doodles: Or, things I already drew

*

One rainy day I was stopped for running a red light
I told the cop I didn't see the light because
my windshield wiper was broken
He gave me two tickets

*

Crazy Americans

*

We wake to rustling in the leaves
A flock of human babies forage
among new shoots

The shepherd, a wizened mutant, guards the perimeters
from ravaging crocodiles

Life is easy in the redwoods

*

The velvet night
The orange rose

*

Chiqui the dog likes Cheerios
with his morning coffee

        September fog crisis
     I miss those voices

I used to write everything until Joanne said,
"You don't have to write everything."
        NOW I can't write anything. . .

Terri takes Chiqui for a walk
He likes to go for a walk after his morning coffee

       Three deer in an oak leaf crush

"The Earth's shadow will creep across
the moon's surface early Tuesday, slowly eclipsing it
and turning it shades of orange and red."

"Don LaFontaine has the rare distinction of being
influential yet invisible."

I look for some sloppy personality footprint
Something stinky in the verse like greasy bacon
or muenster cheese

Familiar bad logic, stigma obsession, redundancy. . .

      Velvet stars, cherry blossoms & peanuts,
                                           proles,
                         deer, bears and Buddha

                *

WHEEL

        Steal apples from neighbor's tree

  "The Gleaners"

      rotavirus

Mea culpa

    hummingbird feeder
    pig mask

        Terri takes the trash out

September 17 at 3:15

BERLIN - Skippi, a wily kangaroo on the run since early August was returned to his home at a petting zoo Monday in southern Germany, after a chase through the German Alps that left the animal with a strained leg.

*

I'm allergic to milk but I'm okay looking at it

*

There's a massive spider web in Lake Tawakoni State Park, Texas
You can hear the mosquitoes screaming

I'm violently attached to my ego

WYOMING, Mich. - A car wash employee got tangled in the giant, automatic brushes and died, authorities said.

"Be careful of the scaffolding," PW

*

A journal (with no dates)
Horrors, terrors and rainbows
A lock of Che Guevara's hair
goes up for auction

*

Luciano Pavarotti goes missing in a song
Antonio Machado stuck in my head

*

The *ficus* tree that grew in my backyard
when I was kid
The one I used to climb all the time
One day I came home and it was gone

*

I don't like change

*

LIFE OF A HARBOR SEAL

"A shark knocks you stupid and you wake up dead."

*

Dogs offer a "semblance" of love

*

A thousand dollars later the hot tub still leaks

The middle class feels guilty
The rich are still shameless

The occupation continues

                    *

Jim says I have an impressive package

                    *

I've got OCD and I don't know
whether to cut my hair or slit my wrists!

"Don't worry," Jim says, "You don't have to choose, you can do them both"

Terri says, "Cut your hair first"

A friend who has OCD writes:

"I'm having trouble piecing together the juxtapositions.
The 1st & 3rd section could fit if I knew more about the 'package.'
Am I missing something? The other thing is that when you say OCD
to me it has a very different weight & meaning
than it does to the average reader. I have OCD up the wazoo.
You're offering humorous OCD that sounds more like
indecisiveness than real OCD. So I find it funny, tongue in cheek,
but so far the strongest relation I see between 1 & 3 is
'throwing the baby out with the bath water,'
which is the whole hog way some OCD folks would operate."

                    *

Reflex tics. . . borderline personality. . .slow gray morning

*

Hysterical propaganda
Apples and honey with Bambi and company

Fall here

Crow, sorrel, pink rose
Civil war, moon walk
Neo-Nazis in Israel

Tantra, farmer, anarchist

*

Gray-haired hippies in Monte Rio airplane hangar movie house
watch *Sicko* and weep

*

Sunday
Paint the window frame green
Kathy has a surplus of eggplants
But only gives us one

A man and a woman jog through the redwoods
With a large Golden Retriever

Organic chicken and apple sausage
Watch Washington "die-in" protest on TV
Some dead and undead

*

September 17, 2007
9am, Hall of Justice
Jury Summons

Case:
Decide whether repeat sex offender,
convicted twice of rape and having served his time
should go into a mental hospital or be released

Fill out hardship form:
Insomnia, under treatment for a year, difficult to concentrate
Weak bladder, under treatment for about a year,
need to get up 2 or 3 times an hour to pee
Have travel plans to read poetry in Tucson & New Mexico
in two weeks therefore unable to sit in on a long trial

Excused!

Rush out of the room with copy of *Democracy in America*
and *The Journal of Albion Moonlight*

*

Dear K_____,

Don't mind David. He always has this anxious crankiness and it doesn't mean anything at all. Sometimes it makes me tired but I never take it personally. Maybe it's general anxiety disorder. That's what I have. My counselor says he doesn't believe in all that stuff because people are so different. But if I have to have something that's what he thinks I have. So onward,

Love, Michael

*

STILL BEAUTIFUL for TC

Dizzie Gillespie and Joan of Arc wing
through invisible curtains

Squirrel taps the fence
Demands more bird seed

Wake up, Goddammit!

        The congregation kneels
           at the edge of the great chasm

I dive into the aquarium
Read poetry to the sharks

How did transparency get so complicated?

        Foxglove
        Glowworms
        Scorpion on the sink

I discover something permanent
But don't know what to do with it

Various petunias hatch from my skull

What do you believe in?

    *

In Chiricahua Park outside of Bisbee he says, "Enough! Enough! Too much beauty. I can't take it. All the clouds and cacti!" So we go to a rundown, kinda rundown desert town, Douglas, on the border, check how our American money is being spent on fences to keep us in and them out and so forth. Big billboards with methheads dissolving against the desert sky. Drove up to Coronado national monument, gravel road mountain overlook. I got vertigo but kept it quiet mostly. Awesome views of Mexico, road runners, sparrow hawks, agave, desert spoons, ocotillo, black caterpillar, deer, and a black and white lady bug David snatched from my sleeve to make a wish. The poetry reading went well last night. A very sweet crowd of friends, locals. Hospitable and receptive. Today Tucson. Stop in another desert park I can't pronounce.

    *

The nurse says, "Look, I have too much to do to worry about germs."
Is all irony poetry?

*

Solomon Excavation Company: "The King Digs"
"I'm a stranger in paradigm"

Porcupine Wash
Ocotillo

250 miles an hour, dollars a minute
Nothing's been the same since the Beatles broke up

Punk rock desert
Saguaro crucifix

Crazy, craggy, jagged mountains
Tap dancing across the wild and wooly west

Where have all the postcards gone?
"Doing Pilates on the banks of the Ganges."
The pose and poems of yesteryear?
"Postcards meet & merge & mutate,
become one great wall size poster
that you can't mail."

Improvisation takes over

"Cicada Sonata"

*

David sleeps in overdosed on saguaro and cholla forests

*

Road to Moab
Cryptobiotic crust

Snow flurries
Sandstone arches and the sky beyond

Beauty becomes painful and The Void
takes the breath out of us all.

6

Gray Days

1

"You have to see the creek that runs by the house here. I walked it the day before yesterday, steep but short climb up the canyon, waterfalls (the constant sound of this place), maidenhair ferns, scraggly oaks draped with lichens, all kinds of mushrooms, fuchsia calypso orchids. Pristine. It's hard to believe it's right here." from a letter to MM

2

In green company of huge redwoods

Money has come between brothers
Doves strike the window in morning pursuit

The news is cut to pieces, distributed
I complain and stay

The rain finally stops, sun frames
the towering tops of the ever living

Sentinels witness my desperate living
Calypso orchids flame in mulch

Gray face, gray days
Winter hysteria succeeds in flood

Cain perpetuates and Abel blames
Under close examination

The flaw. . .

3

Talk to NY and back

      RE BEAT: post-war dissidents

         "Audition"

            medication

Thurs 9:30am. Dizzy
pigeons coo in the window box

Fri. 1am
82 dozen twitches

      As long as the master lives
      there remains objective evidence
      of a beautiful tradition

blink, blink
blink, blink

4

        Goodnight, Marianne Moore

5

8:45am

    As I get older
    I find the present more compelling

        Walt Whitman's America, David S. Reynolds

      (press ENTER to insert)

Sand grain in my ear
rubs the nerve the wrong way
Vertigo, alarming but not harming

      Sinusitis, caffeine, gospel

        Songs of Langston Hughes

6

Sleepy-morning sore throat

This isn't a gray day but rather an exceptional Spring day

Battle of Seasons

Buds grow
Buds freeze

Grow again
Through hell or high water

Battle for Rome
Bird flu for my rosebud baby!
        What do the White House fleas do?

        Courtly love?
      Condoleeza Rice and Dick Cheney
play hide & seek in the Lincoln bedroom

7

But more than one day, it is two days
One clear then one rainy day
More rain

Another cloudy day
Fill hot tub

      Eat two apples, one banana, not enough
Where are my anxious
peanuts?

   Monocled Mr. Peanut poem
      arrives in the mail from David

           Thank you, dear Orpheus!

   Roasted, please

     _____

Benign Paroxysmal Positional Vertigo

     _____

     March 29 went missing
     in worlds of rain

Keep running, Jonah!

     All! All!
8

Big black umbrella shelters a big red smile

Australian lamb stew w/ red potatoes & carrots
Gravy from the drippings

Chill in my bones

In the room where my son wages a virtual war
the roof leaks in buckets

9

Oh, this aching world!
I must get over it quick!
That mist in the oaks
as thick as fire
It's a pleasure to be an angel

Marianne Moore's regatta of small jinxed boats
Vegetable Kingdom for a brain
Lichen fuzz in my sensibility bush

Anselm sends the Collected Poems of Marianne Moore
I think he knows me better than I thought
Or we just happen to be on the same wave-length

10

        "This is eternity."

    Opaque reshape shift drift drip drip this

As this...

    Grays give me the blues, spring subdued by revolutionary
and reactionary forces, bipartisan conversion, systems beyond Time

    I saw the headlines

BE AFRAID, VERY AFRAID

        Silver blaze MOON bleeds in branches
      hung by invisible difference

                Yellow primrose & forget-me-nots

11

Plastic mouthguard hangs from my mouth, shines with spittle
Screw-eyed look between treetops for blue sky optimism
Disenchanted grunt and my stomach growls
Oh, for the good old hot toddy days
Gone with my liver
Gone with cigarettes and Valium
Aspirations of a novelists, perspiration of a horticulturist
Sparrow skips, flits, pecks seed on the ground
in the squishy garden

12

Ash gray rain on muddy creek

Dirty pink stream blurs pebbled banks
Tears a verse away

        Mist in pine forest
     Copper clouds stutter against aluminum gray sunset

    Blink of day

"Rain, rain, rain," Terri sings from downstairs. . .

           On the line Michael M. sings, "The stream should be your Muse"

13

              I went to see my Muse today
              Lovely, I thought, and full of rain.

End Of January

1

Rain, creak, rush, break
Leak in the roof

Another baptism
Crowns a Jew

Gash and smoke

Bare legs brace and bend
Against a wobbling street

Poetry and silk. . .

2

17,000 slot machines

One quarter: no inspiration
Two dollars: a drop of grace
Ten dollars: a tease, tug, love/hate
Twenty dollars: chance fails

Try the buffet

3

Drive & Park
Park & Sleep
Sleep & Fly
Fly & Fly
& Fly

Go nowhere. Get there
The end

4

Rain and palm trees soak my sleep
Few stars, no moon

Dream
Beyond the breakers
My father navigates an open boat
Without running lights
Through seas to find a restaurant
And runs aground in the shallows

5

Windows fall out of a crumbling head

A naked man on a bicycle points at a broken eye
Skewered by the wind

Puppies scream from a car
Pre-dawn insomnia whiplash

Astroturf gardens populate
Both ends of the world

Until the director says, "Cut"
And sends the cast out for empanadas

6

"Coo-koo"
"Coo-koo"

Translucent blue bottles
A couple dozen Hollywood crows

7

Vegetation sucks at my feet
José Martí, García Lorca, clouds
In the cabbage palm.

Day 4

Dramatized, the dog is now on Bowium

We are headed for the Fiesta of the Lyric Shroud
In our car of skulls, paints and plumes

Keyboards and metaphors
Pierced by authority and affiliation

Scarified by craft, ready to pray
To the priests who feed the oracle

We will drink dry white wine
And slip out back for a puff

We're headed for the celebration
Thorns, pearls, purple robes

Atheistic cross-dressers
With hardening of the arteries

Crows and blackberries
Vineyard rows and redwood groves

Pass them by on our way
To the coronation

The geriatric Feast
Un-sustained

Unable to sustain
The anarchy

Or heal the beast
We're headed to the province

Of arts & crafts, hummus,
And callous daffodils.

Morning Noise

It's Spring again

Wisteria smothers the porch
Pink camellia blossoms wrestle with the roses

The poet wears blue
Recites a prayer in four voices

Dog whines at the door

Caught in a chemical stink
I want to get up and seize the day but can't

There was a suicide then a birth

A coffee shop on the boulevard
where we tried to make up in 10 minutes
what we lost in 40 years

Get ready for the hurricane
The shutters go up

Vendetta shreds old fronds
Uproots the banyan tree

Our inheritance
Our legacy

History on sale at the antique market
Flower girls in Piazza San Marco
Miniature portraits

Angels on stilts

I'm learning to play guitar
So I can follow the melody of another mind
So I can be blind to the deafening attitudes

Sleeping pills help
And those sleepy echoes of light in the eaves

Wheels wobble through a morning deceit

The squirrel wants more peanuts
That dog wants his treat

More work
More Sabbath concessions

Good morning Saturday
What else have you got in store?

Anxiety

Chiqui pukes on the bedroom floor
6am, turn the lights on, clean it up
It's hard to be an old dog
in the redwoods

Cuban coffee
Lots of cream, lots of sugar
Unwinding, rewinding
I can't stop myself

All is good
All is great
I imagine parties and music
Cacti and open roads
Art everywhere
In New Orleans
The shadow of the White House
Not far from Wall St.
I want to go there!

Hell, the tail wags the dog

The law is at my door looking
for illegal aliens
Legal too long I want to go bad
but I care way too much
And so remain convenient

A pearly moon
Bug bites on my knees
Beach walks and feathery seas
Gone entirely without me
I abandon ecstasy for a day job

I want to go out and stay out!

Then I hear my father's voice
"Wait a minute, not so fast!"

I wake and polish the illusion.

New Day

Rain drips on the window
Murderers run free

Happy New Year!

A man with a black and yellow umbrella
Walks through green puddles on the roof

Words in wet stinking ash
In yoke and chains

I am listening for the radiant pulse

On that slippery playground carousel
'Round and 'round

Ping!
Ping!

Pong!

I give myself over to the parade
A temporary truce

But dogs hate the rain

The other day I heard them
Talking about poetry.

Broken

The sky is falling
Free enterprise spawns
a Radiant Future

Hallelujah,
Capitalism!
Obama sells out

The long-nailed dog
Clicks clacks
across the broken floor

Click clack
500,000 murdered globally
every year

78 million acres of forest
go up in smoke
Click clack

A tired aphrodisiac
A pre-fabricated liberal model
Built from chicken parts

We sniff glue
on a day of action
Silence sewn to stuttering mouth

A crowded bouquet
of rainbows twists and bleeds
in heaven's eaves

Praise the Lord!
Someone deserves the credit
Bat-winged bison
and ass-camels trample the corpse

of "Tyger, Tyger"
finally burned out
Hallelujah!
Donations for the cause
are on their way

In the foggy morning rain
we'll migrate to the moon
while Holy Men fart and pray
underwater…

Hallelujah…
Glug, glug
The Electric Beast!
New Age Dybbuk!

Jesus is this season's hurricane
Viral winds toss the fronds
Baptismal puss floods the brain

Humanity sucks!
Hallelujah…
Sometimes things are looking up
But it's a house on fire

Click clack
And my nerves are shot
Ole!
Unhinge the smoky wave

Fish for sweet dreams
in a plastic ocean
In a sinking porcelain ship

It's a toxic nightmare
Suicide stars
on daytime game shows!
"Me! Me! Me! Pick Me!

I want to live in Hollywood
In ten fabulous houses in Aspen
London, Maui and beyond
I'm an American man

I know what life is like!"

Numb sleep in epidemic shadows
Embalmed in passionate satin
I am lost and belong nowhere
Maybe I will roll through

underground tunnels to Israel
Quick revival from a bone called Luz
Oh, desperate sunshower!

Click, clack
Glug, glug

O broken Hope!
O, cliché!

Scaffolding

Fungus
Pulled from dilated earth

Subterranean, Drywood and Dampwood Termites

Wood Boring Beetles and Carpenter Ants
(Be careful of the scaffolding)

New doorknobs
Chinese horses

Brushed nickel, chrome, antique brass
Have you considered paisley?

Mustard and stainless steel

Roots in the leach field
Low pressure sibilant dystopia

Cellular terrorism
(It's enough).

About the Author

Michael Rothenberg is a poet, songwriter, editor and publisher of the online literary magazine Big Bridge, www.bigbridge.org, and co-founder of the global poetry movement 100 Thousand Poets for Change, www.100tpc.org.

Born in Miami Beach, Florida in 1951, Rothenberg moved to the San Francisco Bay Area in 1975 and co-founded Shelldance Orchid Gardens in Pacifica, which is dedicated to the cultivation of orchids and bromeliads. While in Pacifica, he helped lead local environmental actions that stopped major coastal developments that would destroy wildlife habitat.

His poems have been widely published in literary reviews such as *Exquisite Corpse, Mudlark, Golden Handcuffs Review, Jacket, OR, Prague Literary Review, Sycamore Review, Tricycle,* and *Zyzzyva.*

His books of poetry include *Favorite Songs* (Big Bridge Press), *Man/Women* with Joanne Kyger (Big Bridge Press), *The Paris Journals* (Fish Drum Press), *Monk Daddy* (Blue Press), *Unhurried Vision* (La Alameda/University of New Mexico Press), *Choose* (Big Bridge Press), and *My Youth As A Train* (Foothills Publishing), and he is the author of the eco-spy thriller *Punk Rockwell* (Tropical Press).

Michael Rothenberg is editor of several volumes in the Penguin Poets series: *Overtime* by Philip Whalen, *As Ever* by Joanne Kyger, *David's Copy* by David Meltzer, and *Way More West* by Ed Dorn. He is also editor of *The Collected Poems of Philip Whalen* published by Wesleyan University Press.

Indefinite Detention: A Dog Story was first published by Ekstasis Editions in Canada in 2013 and is scheduled for publication in 2014 by Al Kotob Khan (Cairo, Egypt) in an Arabic edition, translated by El Habib Louai.

www.ingramcontent.com/pod-product-compliance
Lightning Source LLC
Chambersburg PA
CBHW081909110426
R18126400002B/R181264PG42743CBX00008B/1